The Fox's Prophecy

The Fox's Prophecy

Poem by D. W. Nash

COMMENTARY BY
R. W. F. POOLE

Illustrations by Diana E. Brown

MICHAEL JOSEPH
LONDON

MICHAEL JOSEPH LTD

Published by the Penguin Group
27 Wrights Lane, London W8 5TZ
Viking Penguin Inc., 375 Hudson Street, New York, New York 10014, USA
Penguin Books Australia Ltd, Ringwood, Victoria, Australia
Penguin Books Canada Ltd, 10 Alcorn Avenue, Toronto, Ontario,
Canada M4V 3B2
Penguin Books (NZ) Ltd, 182–190 Wairau Road, Auckland 10, New Zealand

Penguin Books Ltd, Registered Offices: Harmondsworth, Middlesex, England

First published in this edition in 1995
Copyright commentary © R.W.F. Poole 1995
Copyright illustrations © Diana E. Brown 1995

Typeset in Baskerville Monophoto
Typeset in England by Cambridge Photosetting Services
Printed in England by Clays Ltd, St Ives plc

A CIP catalogue record for this book is available from the British Library

ISBN 0 7181 3879 1

INTRODUCTION

The Fox's Prophecy has always intrigued me. Its provenance has, however, sometimes been in doubt.

In the foreword to the J. A. Allen 1976 edition of the poem, the author is 'unknown' and it goes on to say that the original was found amongst old church papers by the Rev Whatley, Vicar of Aston Ingham in Gloucestershire. There was no author's name, just the words 'Cheltenham 1871' at the end of the manuscript. This was given in 1889 to William Gordon Canning Esq, then Master of the Ledbury, who produced a limited edition in 1914 in aid of War Charities. The Gordon Canning family produced another edition in 1930 in aid

of the Gloucester
Royal Infirmary.
In a 1918 edition
(produced in aid of the
Red Cross) Thomas
Kingscote states that the
poem was 'found amongst
the papers of the late Mr D. W.
Nash and were (sic) probably written
by him about the winter of 1870–71'.
So it would seem that the origin of the poem may be as elu-
sive as the ghostly Fox.

I am not going to comment about the contents here, as I
am going to be doing it hereafter. But Kingscote goes on to
say: 'At that time the writer was no doubt impressed by the
brilliant military triumphs which Prussia … obtained against
France and possibly his mind was full of forebodings as to
what the rise of a great new and ambitious power like
Germany might mean for England'. The Fox and his creator
were indeed prescient.

There have been various other editions of *The Fox's Prophecy* but, to the best of my knowledge and belief, this is the first one with a commentary. Only you can judge the success of that commentary; all I can say is that it was fun to do and I feel honoured to have been asked to do it.

As the 1918 edition was in aid of the Red Cross, the society was offered a share of the royalties of this latest edition. This was refused on the grounds of Political Correctness, or the lack of it. So the Hunt Servants' Fund will benefit instead. I am sure that the Fox would approve of that.

R. W. F. POOLE
Northumberland, 1994

Tom Hill was Huntsman to the Cotswold Hunt from 1865 to 1868. I know nothing about him, but the Hills were a famous dynasty of Hunt Servants. Devotees of Surtees will know of Tom Hill, Huntsman to the Old Surrey Hunt in the early part of the last century, with whom Mr Jorrocks, the famous sporting grocer of Great Coram Street, was wont to besport himself (see *Jorrocks' Jaunts and Jollities*). Those who have not read the works of Surtees have a treat in store for them. Written around the middle of the last century, his books are not only comedy classics, but acid-sharp social chronicles of their time.

Guiting (Guy-ting) Wood is, well, Guiting Wood. The Guitings are between Cheltenham and Stow-on-the-Wold. There are two of them, Temple Guiting (presumably once a fief of the Knights Templar) and Guiting Power, the provenance of which name I do not know.

TOM HILL was in the saddle,
    One bright November morn,
The echoing glades of Guiting Wood
    Were ringing with his horn.

November is a funny month. In some years it marks the start of winter. In others it sees the coda of autumn with some residual warmth in the sun.

The first frosts whiten the grass and give a gentle foretaste of the times to come when the cold will really grip and bite. For the time being there may be the pleasure of snappy mornings and sunny days that have the smell of early winter, a heady cocktail of rotting leaf, freshly turned earth, dying bracken all mixed, shaken and stirred by the clean winter wind, that rousts the soul and makes you glad to be out and about in it. It obviously stirred the writer and it is a time of year that I always look forward to.

The hare can lie on the fallow again these days, thanks to the ridiculous EC system of set aside. Some large landowners are pulling in seven-figure sums for this lunacy. Not that I blame them. The fact that the system is wrong is not their fault and if you can get more money for milking the system than for milking cows, then good luck to you.

6

The diamonds of the hoar-frost
  Were sparkling in the sun,
Upon the fallen leaves the drops
  Were shining one by one.

The hare lay on the fallow,
  The robin carolled free;
The linnet and the yellow finch
  Twittered from tree to tree.

In stately march the sable rook
  Followed the clanking plough;
Apart their watchful sentinel,
  Cawed from the topmost bough.

Peeped from her hole the fieldmouse
  Amid the fallen leaves;
From twig to twig the spider
  Her filmy cable weaves.

Mr Nash would have been referring to the charming red squirrel which is no longer to be seen in the Cotswolds. It has been driven out by that very nasty American import, the nearly ubiquitous grey squirrel, or tree rat. I am fortunate to live in one of the last strongholds of the red squirrel and see them often when I am about in the woods. Even this stronghold is threatened by the grey tide from both north and south. There is only one way to save the red species and that is by killing the greys, by all known legal means. This should not be too unpalatable to the Great British Public as Beatrix Potter did not write about grey squirrels.

In many ways I equate the plight of the ab-original English countryman with that of the red squirrel. Perhaps we, too, should be protected by all known legal means. If the countryman is to become a protected species, then there will have to be some proper system of predator control.

The waving of the pine boughs,
    The squirrel's form disclose;
And through the purple beech-tops
    The whirring pheasant rose.

The startled rabbit scuttered
    Across the grassy ride;
High in mid-air the hovering hawk
    Wheeled round in circles wide.

The freshest wind was blowing
    O'er groves of beech and oak,
And through the boughs of larch and pine
    The struggling sunbeam broke.

The varied tints of autumn,
    Still lingered on the wood,
And on the leaves the morning sun,
    Poured out a golden flood.

The hare and all wildlife would benefit if set aside could be used for positive conservation purposes. At the time of writing this is not allowed. As I understand it, the Common Agricultural Policy costs every person in the UK something in the region of £1,000 per annum. It is a criminal nonsense and I use 'criminal' advisedly as some of the prime beneficiaries of the CAP are Sicilian concrete overcoat manufacturers and their political chums.

But, enough of this dreary politicising: we are going hunting. It is a good hunting morning with 'enough blue in the sky to mend a Dutchman's breeches'. One of the reasons that I love November is that it is the start of the foxhunting season; what a dreary waste winter would be without it.

Soft, fleecy clouds were sailing,
  Across the vault of blue;
A fairer hunting morning,
  No huntsman ever knew.

All nature seemed rejoicing,
  That glorious morn to see;
All seemed to breathe a fresher life –
  Beast, insect, bird and tree.

It is amazing and might seem impossible that thirty to forty assorted hounds, all singing their hearts out, as they triumph on the scent line of a fox, can suddenly disappear into thin air, but it can and does happen. It can especially happen in a hilly country like the Cotswolds, where the nature of the ground can dictate detours for those following on horses. Hounds can slip round a corner of a fold in hills and disappear from sight and sound as though they had never been. Experience will tell you where you might pick them up, but hounds are following the fox and he is the only one who actually knows where he is going. This is not necessarily where you think he ought to be going.

But sound and sight of beauty,
　　Fell dull on eye and ear;
The huntsman's heart was heavy,
　　His brow oppressed with care.

High in his stirrups raised he stood,
　　And long he gazed around;
And breathlessly and anxiously,
　　He listened for a sound.

A lost huntsman is not a happy teddy. After all, he is supposed to be the engine driver and people expect him to be up in the cab. However, it does happen to all huntsmen from time to time and may occasion a sense of furious panic, especially with the knowledge that habitually lost huntsmen pretty soon become ex-huntsmen. But panic is not the answer. The answer is to pause, calm down, listen and watch. The passage of a pack of hounds does not go unnoticed in the countryside. Hounds may swing back into hearing. The frenzied barking of farm dogs may give a helpful lead. The bunching of sheep on a distant hillside is a useful marker.

It is sometimes better to rely on your own intuition and experience. I can remember arriving lost and lonely on a road to be told by Car A that hounds were in Warmecombe (due north) only to be told by Car B that they were ('certain sure') in The Stobbs (due south). It is small wonder that some huntsmen appear to have split personalities.

But nought he heard save song of bird,
    Or jay's discordant cry;
Or when among the tree tops,
    The wind went murmering by.

No voice of hound, or sound of horn,
    The woods around were mute,
As though the earth had swallowed up,
    His comrades – man and brute.

He thought, I must essay to find,
    My hounds at any cost;
A huntsman who has lost his hounds
    Is but a huntsman lost.

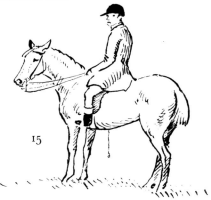

We may assume that our huntsman is in a fairish taking by this time and that the sight of a fox will be as balm to his soul. He would reason that where a fox would be, then his hounds might not be far behind. Unless, of course, it was a fresh fox, in which case its appearance would not be a help. Whatever, the last thing that a huntsman wants to do in a situation like this is to start shouting his fool head off and blowing a trumpet voluntary. Remember the old adage that noise has saved the lives of more foxes than almost anything else. Still and all, most of us do silly things in moments of frustration and excitement. There are few things more exciting than seeing a fox.

However, there is more to this fox than meets the eye, as we shall discover shortly.

Then round he turned his horse's head,
   And shook his bridle free,
When he was struck by an aged fox,
   That sat beneath a tree.

He raised his eyes in glad surprise,
   That huntsman keen and bold;
But there was in that fox's look
   That made his blood run cold.

Silver and even white foxes do occur occasionally in the British Isles. I have never seen one in the flesh, but I have seen a silver-grey pelt. Here we are dealing with a supernatural fox and one that speaks, so it is entitled to be any colour that it wants to be.

There were two old friends who for many years shot, fished and hunted together. One of them went bald whilst the other retained his fine head of hair, although his pelage became as grey as a badger. The two men arranged for a fishing holiday together, then the full-headed one died just before the holiday started. The survivor was going to cancel the trip but was persuaded to go by the widow. 'You know that Gilbert would want you to go.' So he went. And later he told her: 'I had no sooner made my first cast, when I saw this damned great grey fox on the other bank, just sitting there staring at me. I shouted at him but he never moved – he just sat there.' It seems that the fox continued to sit until the fisherman got into a sea trout. When he finally landed it, the fox was gone '…and I said, "Thank you, Gilbert." And never saw the fox again.'

Foxes are strange animals.

18

He raised his hand to touch his horn,
　　And shout a 'Tally-Ho!'
But, mastered by that fox's eye,
　　His lips refused to blow.

For he was grim and gaunt of limb,
　　With age all silvered o'er;
He might have been an Arctic fox,
　　Escaped from Greenland's shore.

But age his vigour had not tamed,
　　Nor dimm'd his sparkling eye,
Which shone with an unearthly fire –
　　A fire could never die.

And thus the huntsman he addressed,
　　In tones distinct and clear,
Who heard as they who in a dream,
　　The fairies music hear.

I am not sure
that speaking
'like a Christian
man' would be
much of a recom-

mendation these days when Christian
leaders fail to make as much sense as Balaam's Ass. Whether
the churches made much more sense in 1870 is a matter for
conjecture, but at least people thought that they did. I suppose
that we may assume that Mr Nash's Christian (I had always
thought that Mr Nash was a clergyman, but there is no
mention of it in the introduction) would be Anglican.

The Church of England was a power and influence in those
days, instead of the minor cult that it has now become. All
those sad, drip-dry bishops should have been chucked out of
the House of Lords long since and then pelted with Series 1
prayer books, or whatever it is they call the castrated version
of Cranmer's masterpiece. I was neither surprised nor shocked
by the ordination of women. After all, the Church has been
ordaining paederasts for years. I prefer women.

'Huntsman,' he said – a sudden thrill,
  Through all the listener ran,
To hear a creature of the wood,
  Speak like a Christian man –

'Last of my race, to me 'tis given,
  The future to unfold,
To speak the words which never yet,
  Spake fox of mortal mould.

'Then print my words upon your heart,
  And stamp them on your brain,
That you to others may impart
  My prophecy again.

You certainly need 'strong life' to be a professional huntsman. The hours are long and the work is both physically and mentally demanding and often dangerous. Long hard hours in the saddle require great physical fitness and stamina. The successful hunting of a fox with a pack of hounds needs computer-like concentration. For all that, it is a healthy life (outwith falls, broken bones and torn muscles – all part of the job).

Long hours out in all weathers can distress your complexion. The tabloid cliché of 'red faced huntsmen' does have a basis in fact. I remember being told by a cheeky chit of a TV make-up girl that I had an expensive face. I replied that it was the result of forty years of weathering. She dismissed that with a sniff and said that she went 'horse riding every Saturday for an hour and her face did not look like mine' – she should have been so lucky.

'Strong life is yours in manhood's prime,
    Your cheek with heat is red,
Time has not laid his finger yet
    In earnest on your head.

'But ere your limbs are bent with age,
    And ere your locks are grey,
The sport that you have loved so well
    Shall long have passed away.

Some explanation required here: 'Colmore' = Mr Cregoe Colmore of Charlton Kings, near Cheltenham, who was Master of the Cotswold Hounds 1858–71. In those palmy days, the MFH was responsible for all the expenses of his hunt with, perhaps, some financial assistance from wealthy followers such as 'The Rendcombe baronet' – Sir Francis Goldsmid, Bart – Sir Alexander Ramsay, Bart., and Mr W. Watson.

The Fox was wrong in part. Cotswold foxes still hear 'the latest huntsman's horn'. The Cotswold have been blessed with some great foxhunters in the mastership – Lt. Col C. Heber-Percy, Capt R. E. Wallace and Sir Hugh Arbuthnot. The 'latest huntsman', well, since 1971, is the great Mr Tim Unwin – a fine huntsman and hound breeder and the biggest eater you will ever see – when his wife is not looking.

'In vain shall generous Colmore
    Your hunt consent to keep;
In vain the Rendcombe baronet
    With gold your stores shall heap.

'In vain Sir Alexander,
    And Watson keen in vain,
O'er the pleasant Cotswold Hills
    The joyous sport maintain.

'Vain all their efforts; spite of all
    Draws nigh the fatal morn,
When the last Cotswold fox shall hear
    The latest huntsman's horn.

To say that a fox feels 'fear' when hunted is to anthropomorphise the fox. Animals do not have imagination. That is what makes the human animal different from the rest. If you watch a hunted fox you will see him stop and listen every now and then. It is the noise of the hounds that instinctively drives him on. If he hears nothing behind him then he will slacken his pace, or even stop and have a scratch.

At one time the Earls of Berkeley hunted a country that stretched from Charing Cross to the Severn. This period is still remembered in Cockney rhyming slang – 'Berk' being a shortened version of 'Burkley Hunt' which is c.r.s. for the *pudenda mulieris*, except that it does not rhyme in Latin.

The Cotswold Hunt began in 1858 after that part of the Berkeley country had been given up by Earl Fitzhardinge (the Earldom of Berkeley finished in 1807). Harry Ayres was the Earl's huntsman. Charles Turner was his first Whipper-in and became the first huntsman to the new Cotswold pack.

Earls may be inclined to flashes of temperament and more especially if they are retired colonels, as this one was.

'Yet think not, huntsman, I rejoice
    To see the end so near;
Nor think the sound of horn and hound
    To me a sound of fear.

'In my strong youth which numbers now
    Full many a winter back,
How scornfully I shook my brush
    Before the Berkeley Pack.

'How oft from Painswick Hill I've seen
    The morning mist uncurl,
When Harry Ayres blew the horn
    Before the wrathful Earl.

'How oft I've heard the Cotswold's cry,
    As Turner cheered the pack,
And laughed to see his baffled hounds,
    Hang vainly on my track.

The Fox is saying what all countrymen know, that foxes prosper in a well-conducted hunting country. Those who would contest this fact might like to ponder the following anecdote.

There was a much publicised parliamentary challenge to hunting by a Labour MP called Macnamara. Just before it was defeated, I was hunting in a lovely valley, which is full of foxes. I asked one of the shepherds who make up the scattered population of the valley what would happen if hunting was banned. His grim reply was that there would not be a live fox left in the valley – if there was not hunting to keep the fox population within reasonable bounds and limit the damage at lambing time, then the foxes would not be tolerated.

You've heard that one before? Facts need constant airing.

'Then think not that I speak in fear,
    Or prophesy in hate;
Too well I know the doom reserved,
    For all my tribe by fate.

'Too well I know, by wisdom taught,
    The existence of my race
O'er all wide England's green domain,
    Is bound up with the Chase.

There are many facts of life and death that those opposed to hunting refuse to face: the alternative methods of killing foxes is a good example. I wonder if you have ever come across a fox dragging its back end along after it has been shot at and gangrene has set in? You would not like it.

I once, very gingerly, opened up an earth in which a vixen and her cubs had been gassed. The old girl had come up the tunnel to meet the poisonous invader. She died with her mouth set in a terrible rictus and oozing a foul green slime. She had not died well. A fox hunted by hounds either dies quickly and cleanly or gets away. You've heard that one before? Facts need constant airing.

It is unfortunate that facts have little to do with much of the opposition to hunting. This opposition is usually based on emotion and sentiment, which are so often used as substitutes for real kindness. There is also the fine old Cromwellian tradition of stopping other people doing things just because you do not like or understand them. This shows that there is nothing new about Political Correctness: it has its roots deep in Prodnose Puritanism.

'Better in early youth and strength
    The race for life to run,
Than poisoned like the noxious rat,
    Or slain by felon gun.

'Better by wily sleight and turn
    The eager hound to foil,
Than slaughtered by each baser churl,
    Who yet shall till the soil.

The Fox, who is now embarking on his prophetic phase, very properly considers that hunting is part of the warp and woof of England. Its decline and  demise would represent a ripping up of the fabric of traditional way of life. This is exactly what certain sections of modern society want. The old saying, 'If it ain't broke, don't mend it' has gone out of fashion.

Those of us who maintain the old habits of sartorial nattiness are liable to be discriminated against. I recently attended an interview at the BBC for a front man for a rural programme. I wore a town suit and a tie. Both hair and moustache were neatly brushed. My appearance was a grave error of judgement. I was dismissed as being 'too Sandhurst'.

'For not upon these hills alone,
    The doom of sport shall fall;
O'er the broad face of England creeps,
    The shadow on the wall.

'The years roll on, old manners change,
    Old customs lose their sway;
New fashions rule; the grandsire's garb
    Moves ridicule today.

It seems that even in 1870 people were worrying about the destruction of the countryside. After two world wars and the Common Agricultural Policy there is certainly a lot more to worry about. After the Hitler War, successive governments encouraged farmers to plant, sow and produce food at all costs. The early days of the CAP continued this trend of heavily subsidised arable cropping on land which was never meant for it. The CAP penny has finally dropped, along with a great deal of taxpayers' money, but the damage done to the countryside by these policies has been immense. I do not know how many acres of woodland or miles of hedgerow have disappeared since 1870, but the Fox would be horrified at the extent of the accuracy of his prophecy.

The 'manly blood' now consists largely of lager, 'illegal substances', and Soya sauce. This mixture is much easier to pump through 'natural gates and alleys' of the human body, which are now well gunged up with cholesterol.

'The woodlands where my race has bred,
  Unto the axe shall yield;
Hedgerow and copse shall cease to shade
  The ever-widening field.

'The manly sports of England
  Shall vanish one by one;
The manly blood of England
  In weaker veins shall run.

'The furzy down, the moorland heath,
  The steam plough shall invade;
Nor park nor manor shall escape –
  Common, nor forest glade.

Events proved the Fox quite correct in his mistrust of the Germans. Churchill rightly described them as being 'either at your feet or your throat'. At the time of writing they seem to have a beady eye on the jugular of Europe yet again. No modern politicians read history, therefore it is hardly surprising that they neglect its lessons – at our collective peril. For instance, it is well to remember that the concept of a 'United Europe' was one of the justifications used by the Vichy government for collaborating with the Germans. Let us not forget how the German/French axis was bred – by Fear out of Treachery.

I would not mind a slice of the 'gilded vice of Gaul', but cannot afford it with a wife, accountant, bank manager and a motley collection of mendicants and camp followers to support. I like the French individually but they are ridiculous as a whole. How can you take seriously a nation that gives the female genital passage a masculine gender – *le vagin*.

'Baser tastes' presumably refers to golf and tennis.

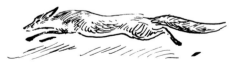

'Degenerate sons of manlier sires
　　To lower joys shall fall;
The faithless lore of Germany,
　　The gilded vice of Gaul.

'The sports of their forefathers
　　To baser tastes shall yield;
The vices of the town displace,
　　The pleasure of the field.

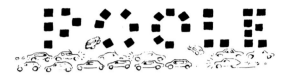

POOLE

'Time-honoured creeds and ancient faiths' are having a roughish time at the moment and 'the ancient landmarks' are sharp disappearing beneath motorways (for Executive tailbacks) and Executive housing (to tailback to). The Fox was spot on. But I wonder if even he envisaged a society in which a Barratt Show House may well become a listed building – New Britain's answer to Blenheim Palace.

I wonder, also, if the Fox had in mind and second sight the appalling contortions by which the Church of England has somehow managed to stick its own knee in its own crutch.

The House of Windsor plc has certainly seen its stock plummet, partly through its own mismanagement, but also because of the envy and hatred whipped up by the 'base churls' of the tabloid press. This is a pity. The Monarchy may not be perfect but it is infinitely preferable to the alternatives – as it might be President Murdoch.

'For swiftly o'er the level shore
   The waves of progress ride;
The ancient landmarks one by one
   Shall sink beneath the tide.

'Time-honoured creeds and ancient faith,
   The Altar and the Crown,
Lordship's hereditary right,
   Before that tide go down.

'Base churls shall mock the mighty names,
   Writ on the roll of time;
Religion shall be held a jest,
   And loyalty a crime.

39

The Fox would be very lucky to find many village schools now and one would be grateful for a little utilitarianism in modern educational practice, which seems to be based entirely on soggy political theory. It does not seem to matter if the children cannot read, write, or count to 10. I do not suppose that the Fox would have believed the case of the new woman teacher in one of the main dairying areas in England who told her charges that it was cruel to milk cows. She left in a hurry and a small motor car. As my informant, a parent and dairy farmer, put it – 'I tell 'ee what, Boy, us fair made 'er udder judder.'

It is interesting how the Fox foresaw the rise of all the phoney cults, 'ologies and 'isms that people swarm round like maggots. 'Self-made apostles' succeed by supplying people with slogans they can mouth mindlessly: it is so much easier than thinking.

'No word of prayer, no hymn of praise
    Sound in the village school:
The people's education
    Utilitarians rule.

'In England's ancient pulpits
    Lay orators shall preach
New creeds, and free religions
    Self-made apostles teach.

We do not have much in the way of peasants these days. Robin Page and I are probably the only people in England who cheerfully admit to peasant status. This is a pity. It is an honourable position in society, as any French politician will tell you; they jump to attention whenever the peasants say 'Boo!'

For prime examples of tasks being fallen to in surly silence, travel on the London Underground in the rush hour with glum-faced passengers packed like sardines in their own oleaginous outpourings. Even the far-seeing Fox could hardly have anticipated such misuse of human body and soul. If you transported animals like that then the 'cruelty people' would certainly, and rightly, be breathing down your neck. 'Gold' is the only thing that can make people put up with that sort of nastiness.

'The peasants to their daily tasks
   In surly silence fall;
No kindly hospitalities
   In farmhouse or in hall.

'Nor harvest feast nor Christmastide
   Shall farm or manor hold;
Science alone can plenty give,
   The only god is Gold.

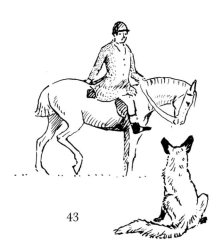

What a far-sighted Fox he was to have foreseen all the ghast-
liness of Feminism and Political Correctness, where women
find it necessary to shave their heads and F and Blind like
Billingsgate porters to try to prove that they are as good as
men. Then you have 'Differently Sexually Orientated' men
frolicking gaily about Hampstead Heath trying to be as good
as women. And what about school teachers who dare not
comfort a crying child, lest they be accused of 'abuse'. Lord
have mercy on us. But to get all of this nonsense in perspec-
tive, you have to stand back and look at modern urban society
with the trained eye of an experienced stockman,
then you will see these aberrations for what they
are – classic stress symptoms. They are the
human equivalent of intensively-kept pigs biting
each other's tails off and the feather pecking of
battery hens. Put humans in unnatural condi-
tions and they will be like the poor buzzard I
saw in a French zoo – mewing and bloodying
its head against the bars of its tiny cage trying
to reach its free cousins soaring above it.

'The homes where love and peace should dwell
    Fierce politics shall vex,
And unsexed woman strive to prove
    Herself the coarser sex.

45

One sometimes wonders whether the affairs of state might not be better left to mechanics in their workshops. That special sucking of the teeth that all mechanics learn when listening to a potentially expensive noise in your car, would make a good substitute for the Budget Statement. You know that both are going to bring you pain and grief, but at least the sharp intake of breath has the virtue of brevity and it would not take up the whole afternoon on a hunting day.

Those who tighten the tappets in the great workshop of government are not very skilled, I fear. In fact, there are those who go so far as to describe our political mechanics as true disciples of Onan (Genesis 38–9). This is not surprising when you consider that most of them are failed second-hand car salesmen, or school teachers who could not teach you how to eat a bacon butty. The only certain thing is that they will cost you a lot of money, Squire – now suck your teeth.

'Mechanics in their workshops
  Affairs of State decide;
Honour and truth – old-fashioned words –
  The noisy mob deride.

I suppose that the 'coarsest demagogue' of present times was Mrs Thatcher. She chucked all the genuine Conservatives out of her government and handed the party over to the spivs. It has become a real Tory party. The Fox could have told you that the word Tory is derived from the Gaelic *Toiridhe* = thief. In case Labour and the Lib Dems should be starting to preen themselves, let it be clear that I regard both parties as vermin pits – crawling with envy, malice and class hatred.

And whilst we are talking in the Gaelic, let us not forget those other arch 'Tories' – the Moguls of the Media. Few people have done more to poison the waterholes of this country. These clever and cynical men are motivated by a lust for power (the ultimate perversion) and riches. The pursuit of wealth is not a bad thing in its self, if (like sex) it is sought after as a means of attaining contentment and happiness. But if sex and wealth are striven for as an end in themselves, then they become perversions. There are many twisted people in public life who regard the public as inflatable dolls to be pumped up and 'used according'.

You may like to think that this is a foul disgrace.

'The statesmen that should rule the realm
    Coarse demagogues displace;
The glory of a thousand years
    Shall end in foul disgrace.

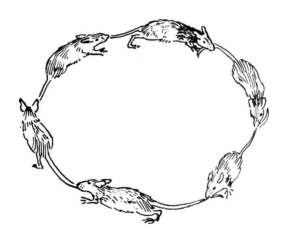

You have to remember that the prophecy was written when Britain was at, or was approaching, the zenith of her imperial might: when the British Army was painting red bits all over the world and the Navy was enforcing the Pax Britannica on 'lesser breeds beneath the sun'. As it turned out we would have been much better off if 'trade had been held the only good'. We should have taken the money and run. We finished up with an Empire and a permanent fiscal haemorrhage.

Did the Fox foresee the day when maintaining a single battalion of troops in the Balkans would make the Army dangerously overstretched and high-quality front line service personnel would be thrown on the scrap heap so that the government could proclaim a spurious 'peace dividend'.

If we had stuck to trade and not sent out all those District Commissioners to impose our concept of righteousness, we should now be rich and boring like the Swiss. Hands up all those who would like to be rich and boring? It beats being grey, shabby and broke.

'The honour of old England,
    Cotton shall buy and sell,
And hardware manufacturers
    Cry "Peace! – lo! all is well."

'Trade shall be held the only good,
    And gain the sole device;
The statesman's maxim shall be peace,
    And peace at any price.

'Her army and her navy
    Britain shall cast aside;
Soldiers and ships are costly things,
    Defence an empty pride.

Well, lookee here! If this ain't the ol' EC the Fox is talking about, then Helmut Kohl is a Brummie. There is little doubt that the Germans would like the EC to do for them what two world wars could not, with the French poodle trailing along behind, still snarling about Agincourt and Waterloo (oh yes they do – I was reminded that the English burned Joan of Arc when I was last in France – but the French brought the firewood, I said). There are many in this country who are licking their lips at the prospect of sticking their snouts into the lovely trough of taxpayers' money that is the European Ideal. To achieve this lip-smacking happiness they will cheerfully sacrifice all and any amount of British sovereignty and independence. Our politicians are handing over *our* money by the sackload to finance a European rape of Britain such as we have not seen since 1066. I am not so sure about the Muscovite, but bears and Russians are very unpredictable.

'The German and the Muscovite
    Shall rule the narrow seas;
Old England's flag shall cease to float
    In triumph on the breeze.

'The footsteps of the invader
    Then England's shore shall know,
While home-bred traitors give the hand
    To England's every foe.

'Disarmed before the foreigner,
    The knee shall humbly bend,
And yield the treasures that she lacked
    The wisdom to defend.

Now the Fox is looking
into our future and one
can only hope that he is right. He
seems to be prophesying our withdrawal
from the EC, but it does look as though it may get worse before
it gets better. The 'disaster' may well be that we are going to
get comprehensively shafted by our European partners to the
extent that even Sir Edward Heath may have to admit that
the whole ghastly business was a mistake (a large pig has just
flapped by my window). The Fox also seems to suggest that
before the Queen's 'crown shall fall, there are crowns to be
broke' (Bonnie Dundee). However, if that is what it takes to
recover national sanity and sovereignty, then let us take the
claymore out of the thatch and get to it. Let our slogan be
'European on my boot!'

'But not for aye – yet once again,
    When purged by fire and sword,
The land her freedom shall regain
    To manlier thoughts restored.

'Taught wisdom by disaster,
    England shall learn to know
That trade is not the only gain
    Heaven gives to man below.

'The greed for gold departed,
    The golden calf cast down
Old England's sons again shall raise
    The Altar and the Crown.

'Rejoicing seas shall welcome
    Their mistress once again;
Again the banner of St George
    Shall rule upon the Main.

Could it be that they are going to send the Franco-German Brigade after us after our withdrawal? Or is Mr Clinton going to have yet another brilliant stab at foreign policy and drop the 101st Airborne on us (perhaps mistaking us for Bosnia – well, we both begin with B and the poor chap does come from Arkansas)? Whatever, it looks as though what remains of the British Army – probably the Household Cavalry Mounted Regiment and the sole remaining Foot Guards Battalion (we kept them for the tourists, you know) is going to do the business.

What then? The Fox seems to suggest that we should return to the old-fashioned values of courtesy, honesty and neighbourliness, the old rural values that are still just hanging on. Thank God. The Fox believes, as I do, that the countryside is the true soul of Britain.

'The blood of the invader
    Her pastures shall manure;
His bones unburied on her fields
    For monuments endure.

'Again in hall and homestead
    Shall joy and peace be seen,
And smiling children raise again
    The maypole on the green.

'Again the hospitable board
    Shall groan with Christmas cheer,
And mutual service bind again
    The peasant and the peer.

'Again the smiling hedgerow
    Shall field from field divide;
Again among the woodlands
    The scarlet troop shall ride.'

The cry of hounds brings an end to the Fox's Prophecy, but I think that you will agree that it was pretty remarkable and thought-provoking stuff. Although it was written at the time of the Franco-Prussian war and with the rising might of Prussia in mind, a lot of the prophecy has indeed come to pass.

Of course, you may wish to dismiss the whole thing as a load of nonsense, but you are perfectly entitled to this point of view. You are also entitled to fit the prophecy to your own ideas and prejudices, just as I have done. All the same, if it makes you think, then it was worth the trouble and, like the Huntsman, as he galloped off to find his hounds, it might just make you shake your head. I wonder what sort of summary would go with this poem in 2070. I do not think that I would like to prophesy – that is best left to Foxes.

Again it seemed that aged fox
    More prophecies would say,
When sudden came upon the wind
    'Hark forrard! Gone away!'

The listener startled from his trance –
    He sat there all alone;
That well-known cry had burst the spell,
    The aged fox was gone.

The huntsman turned, he spurred his steed,
    And to the cry he sped;
And, when he thought upon that fox,
    Said naught, but shook his head.

SOMERSET
Photographs by Bob Croxford

Published by Atmosphere Publishing Ltd
Mullion Cornwall TR12 7DF
Tel 01326 240180
www.atmosphere.co.uk

ISBN 978-0-9550805-5-5

Cover THE SOMERSET LEVELS

CHEDDAR GORGE

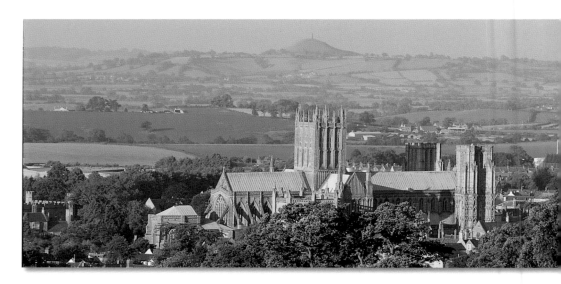

WELLS CATHEDRAL with GLASTONBURY TOR in the distanc

CATHEDRAL GREEN, WELLS

The exterior of WELLS CATHEDRAL'S astronomical clock

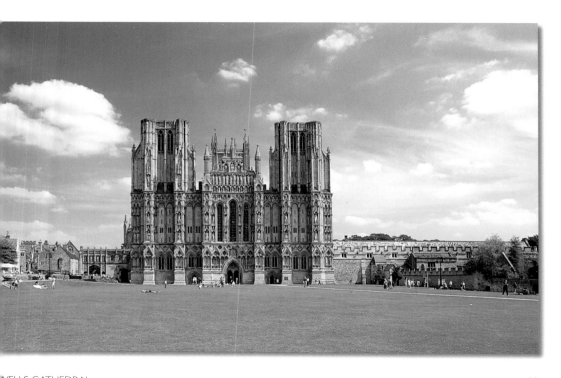

The magnificent West Front of WELLS CATHEDRAL

The evocative ruins of GLASTONBURY ABBEY

GLASTONBURY TC

The GLASTONBURY THORN

Sunset over GLASTONBURY TOR

On top of GLASTONBURY TOR

Dawn breaks over GLASTONBURY TOR

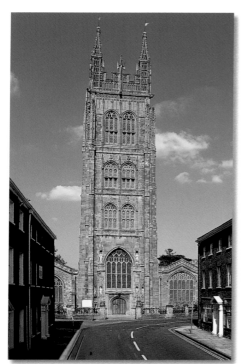

St Mary Magdalene Church, TAUNTON

TAUNTON CASTLE home of The Museum of Somerset

Harvesting apples for Somerset's famous cider

BURROWBRIDGE MUMP

THE LEVELS, North Drain near Wedmore

ollarded trees near BURROWBRIDGE MUMP

Butleigh Moor, THE LEVEL

CHEDDAR MOOR looking towards THE MENDIPS

HE LEVELS in the mist

WITHYPOOL in the Barle Valley

WATERSMEET, Exmoor

TARR STEPS, Exmoor

DUNSTER CASTLE

DUNSTER CASTLE overlooks the Yarn Market

EXMOOR PONIES

LORNA DOONE country, Exmoor

THE ROYAL CRESCENT, BATH

Meeting in THE ABBEY CHURCHYARD, BATH

PULTENEY BRIDGE, BATH

Looking towards BREAN DOWN on the Bristol Channel coast

THE GRAND PIER at WESTON-SUPER-MAR

STEMBRIDGE TOWER MILL

INDEX

The sword in the stone, TAUNTON CASTLE